Moonlight

Nimit Suri

i

To the one with whom I fell in love at first sight ...
'My Mother'

CONTENTS

POET'S DILEMMA

If I haven't borne this pain
How can I sing it with purity?

INTRODUCTION

One who wishes to love finds no one to receive
One who wishes to be loved finds no one to give,
Yet in this strange world everyone seeks love

Being in love is a delightful experience, but sadly love also brings along agony and hurt. The more deeply you suffer in love the more difficult it is to love again. However, what good is a life without love and hurt? A guarded person living a dreary life once remembered his first engagement with love;

How I wish to be in love again,
Like once it seized my virgin heart
Intoxicated, I wandered into a blissful paradise

How I wish to be tormented by love again,
Like once it set my heart on fire
Mournful, I suffered in boundless agony

How I wish to experience love in such extremes

Regretfully, after every fall, we are more cautious and our willingness to lose ourselves in someone reduces and so does the pain experienced with loss. But what good is that love which is wary of hurt? In my poems, I have endeavored to capture such profound ironies and evoke relatable emotions in anyone who has ever been touched by love.

 Poetry in this book is divided into four sections, **In love, Falling Apart, Agony** and **Falling In love again** to capture myriad feelings of love in all its essence. I wish readers a delightful and profound reading experience.

Nimit

MOONLIGHT

In Love...

And we kissed,
A delicious poison shot through my lips
A charming ruin beset my heart

His gentle touch lit the dark alleys,
where she guarded with care,
her inflammable desires

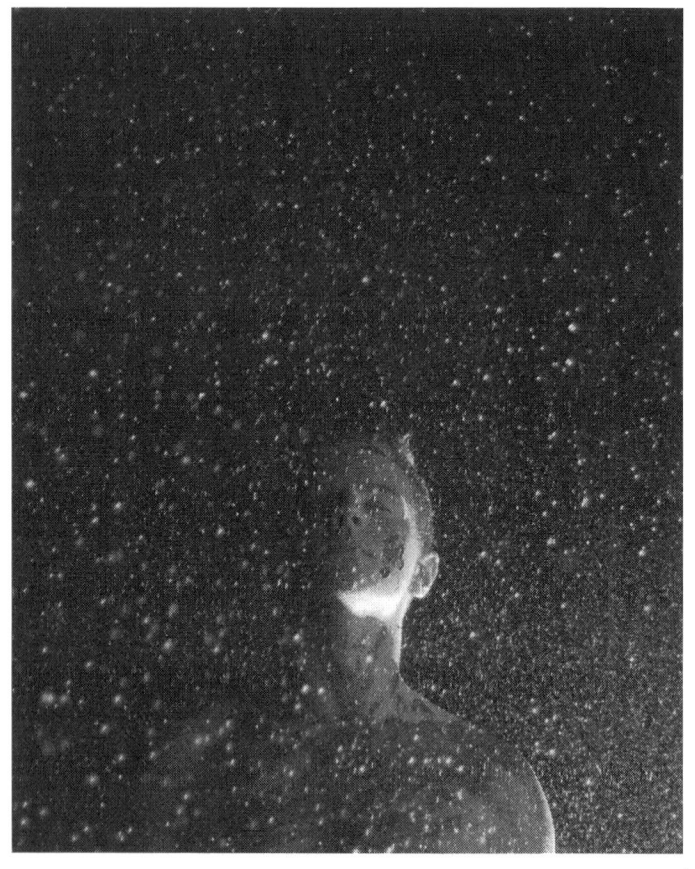

I have more in my heart than what i say,
and more in my desires
than what my lips convey

'I Love You'

An old chestnut

A cliché

Oh spirit of my heart,

allow me the riddance of these words ,

for they hardly convey what I feel for you

You are a wordsmith,

braiding moons and stars

A deceptive angel of an elusive paradise,

A crafty charmer putting me to sin,

Oh I know the nightmare I will wake to,

But for now,

I wish to live the dream I am in

I live with a desire to possess
not her
but her tender heart
For, I may put a nightingale in a cage
but I cannot make her sing

She trembles on my touch
beckons when I move away
She kisses me deep
spews cuss afterwards
Her words are bitter
breath soft and sweet
Morning she is a stranger
night she leaves strawberries on my tongue

This exhausting chaos and your warm embrace

A world drunk on hate and your lips to sober up

We lay there gazing at the stars,
listening to the song of waves,
bonded in purity,
Silence as language of the hearts

Birds sang melodies
enchanting flute played,
Aromas lingered in the air
while we melted in embrace,
Unwound- You, me and existence
played a beautiful symphony

Her lips poured an exquisite wine,

Every sip pushing me into slumber

I am here walking by the sea,
drowned in heavenly thoughts
of you and me
In solitude, amidst the crowd around
In peace with chaos that surrounds
Praise your love
that liberates me from trivialities
and worries of the day
Barefoot against the setting sun
as I stroll my way

Crushed under a compelling desire
Lips delighted in bliss
Dazed, they forged an eternal bond

I hear a whisper,

silk slithering on skin

I see an angel

sweet scent lingers

A subtle touch, growing desire

Fleeting but indelible, this lovely moment

This separation must not be cursed,
through this I have known longing

A longing that must be endured,
to understand the depths of this thirst

A thirst that must be quenched slowly,
to experience the extreme delight
when intense passions are satiated

And passions should never be completely doused,
so this heart forever kindles in love

I bear this distance,
In the hope of your unwavering promise
towards me
To soothe you from pain of my absence
and remind you of our inseparable bond
I send you this little note of love

It is the torment of your beauty
that I may touch but cannot hold
A brief kiss
that soothes my senses
but cannot be preserved
Your love that cannot be guarded
for it is free
Yet it subtly places me in your captivity

'Kiss'

With closed eyes

I try to savor this fleeting moment of pleasure

It is a passing wonder

that brings me few drops

from the boundless ocean of love

concealed in the depths of her heart

This morning
I woke up
with tender heart and butterflies in stomach

Thank you love
for another beautiful day

MOONLIGHT

Falling Apart..

Some bonds are bondages

Ironical that

certain weakness

makes me bear his mess

and

he calls me

Pillar of his strength

A baggage of words remains
some spoken to cause hurt
some unspoken to show love

Strange is this longing that refuses to die
You fill me with love yet I am unsatisfied

Depth of her heart
was not entirely concealed
had he noticed
his lost reflection in her eyes

Every time you praised my pretenses
and blamed my virtues,
My loneliness with you grew

I wish your love was liberating
But your thoughts became my words
and your words became my actions

Friends were not enough
She longed for love
But then love wasn't enough either
So she longed for friends

Helpless in love
She crawled
like a shadow of the demon
who possessed her
Leashed, in straits
A desire to fly with clipped wings,
A dream to live in parched eyes,
A hope of love in a broken heart

A desire to sail
but with a foot on land,
A wish to dive deep
but with an eye on sky.
To the creed of such nerveless wanderers
love owes its hurt

What good is your truth
that is told to confess the lies
You are the murderer
and you bring me news of the dead

And the gods wondered,
A gift of words bestowed upon them
But pity how these words are played,

Used with deception to praise,
Applied with sincerity to bleed

A
foolish desire for freedom,
To cut the rope from one end,
only to tie it to another

Time to leave was long gone,
yet she stayed
until her scars were etched deep
Perhaps, to reach a point beyond forgiveness

He could fill a side of her bed
but not her voids
His presence reminded how lonely she was

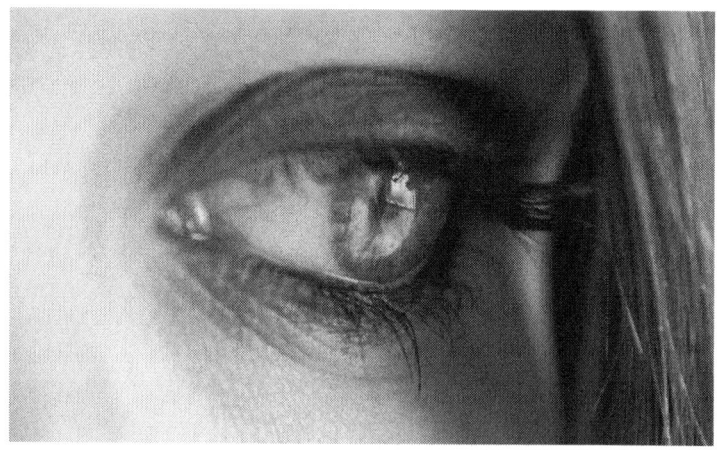

I see
that you had me enough
and do not want me anymore
When I can willfully give
the freedom you desire,
Why is it important for you
to put me at fault?

Perhaps you are right
'I will find someone better'
But this is a pity I don't deserve
And you may be right that
'You don't deserve me'
But this is an insult
you do not deserve

Agony...

Wistful moment of pride
took her away
Apologies not tendered
frozen on the lips
Arms refusing the embrace
that heart yearned to give
Some memories to cherish
but many regrets to live

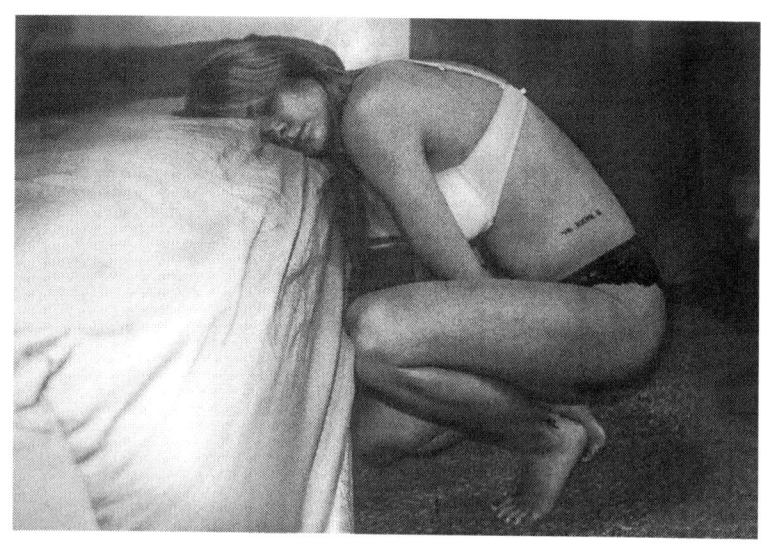

Rueful moment of desperation
when he let me go
Waited for few words
but they never flowed
I wished to be stopped and held tight
Neither I was wrong
nor he was right

Upon his leaving,
Something inside me died
and Something came alive

My heart sinks with the thought
that we may never meet again

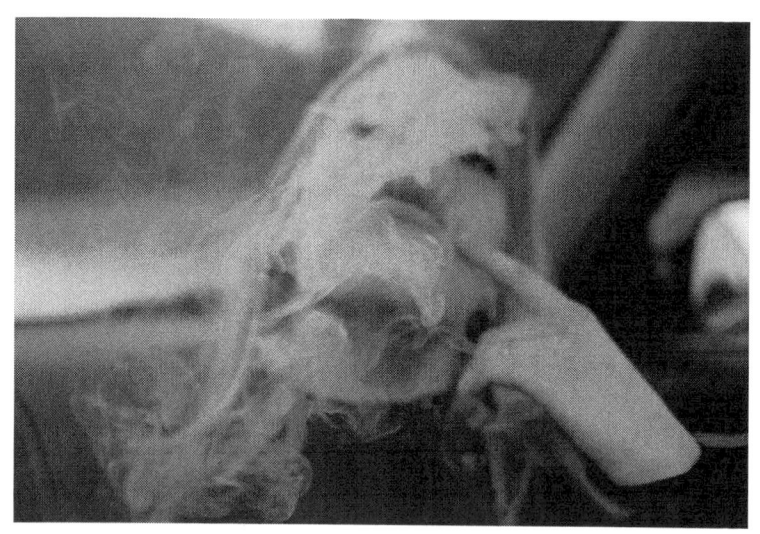

Let me be drowned in spirits,
The reality I escape is more pitiful
than the nightmare I am in

I listen to the cacophony
to drown the clamor inside
Drink wine to smother the overwhelming thoughts
And then with haphazard motions of body,
I join the crowd of desolates
in a grand pretense of celebrations

She caged her crippled heart
behind the walls of steel
And walked past everything blissful
calling herself free

It wasn't love she sought
but a relief
from the skeletons of past
that rattled her mind

As she lay besides a man
undressed and desolate,
She reasoned the reckless acts of intimacy
as her brief escape

It is her body he relished
but her heart is for none,
tender part of her soul
was ravaged by someone

Night she posed as a beloved
in most passionate way
but then, a self-seeking harlot
when woke by morning ray

To save her,
defiant she walked
naked- from head to toe

amidst the lecherous crowd
that leered and cheered

She acquired abused hurled
as language of freedom she desired

Like stars she wore her scars
to be liberated of pain she expected

Love made her weak
so she always answered Love
with indifference

A charming wanderer knocked

sought comfort on his way,

Briefly rented my heart

with no intent to stay,

Smoothly won my love

and cowardly walked away

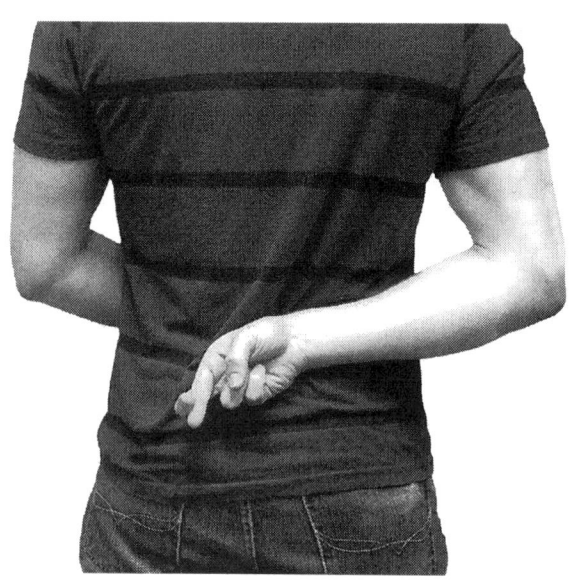

Perhaps truth in the word 'love'
needs reinforcement now

That is why people call it
'True Love'

Where others tried to save their souls,
I decided to bare mine

How tenderly, I unveiled the feelings of my heart
How cruelly you turned and walked away

Love tested her twice;
Once when he left
and then when he returned

Between the pages
of my cherished book
lay a dry rose,
that once blossomed with splendor

Now faded, brittle and
bereft of sweet fragrance
that I failed to preserve,

From dawn to dusk
this rose has lived our love story

I may forgive a mistake
but not a betrayal,
I may overlook a lie
but not a deceit

Certain weakness makes me stay
but I may never love again

As she nursed her wounds
and prepared herself
She realized that love has failed
to preserve the good in her

With all her heart,
She was set to destroy
the one she loved,
with all her heart

For days she wore his unwashed shirt
preserved in her closet

But soon his fragrance disappeared
and it was nothing but a piece of cloth

He who calls me cruel,
the crafty one
my heart refused to accept

Ask yourself,
If it is your heart that is wounded or your ego

Do you suffer from longing
or an agony of unachieved goal?

This is my last ode
to the one
who saw me unworthy of love

If my acknowledging
caused ripples of discomfort at least,
I deserved polite words

Here and Henceforth
I abandon all claims and
move on with a battered heart

Praying for peace to envelop both of us

Falling in love again...

Love be the curse bestowed upon us,
as those immersed in it
are no less miserable
than the ones hurt in it,

Yet this foolish heart
is eager to fall in love again

She was neither in heaven
nor in hell
In a curse of being 'just well'

Enchanted by illusion
inclined but uncertain
to stay inside the wall
or give it all,

She was standing indecisive
at the door of revelation,

Naked she enters
wounded she leaves

I have two hearts,
One is a devoted servant
and other; a terrible master

I am a tiny raindrop
falling into the boundless
Let me embrace a withering leaf,
before I cease to exist

Life is a sort of waiting
for someone I don't know yet

Before you enter
through the door of my heart
tell me honestly
Do you intent to stay?
If not,
I will keep your space that way

No matter how modest,
I prefer deeds over words

For i have often witnessed
snazzy love letters vanish in fire

From those who claim your affection,
hear not what is said
but what is left unsaid

Often lies are sold

through excessive talking

Feelings are best expressed in words just enough

or through silence,

For silence is the language of the hearts

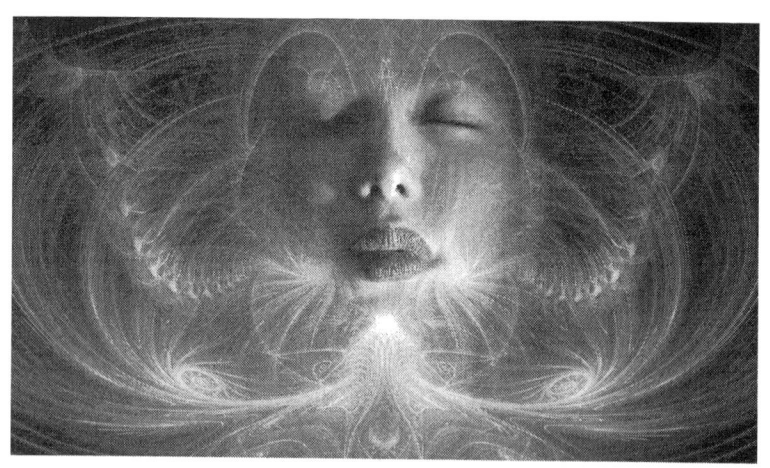

Doused by hurt
but fanned by longing,
embers of love
still smolder inside me

Embrace me , for I fear loneliness,
Hope has kept me waiting for long now

Lay by my side
hold my hands
Stay, Just stay
While I pull myself up
Till I put myself together

Love and pain
embrace both

For one is soul of other
In one sacred fire they kindle

Invite love comes along the pain,
Avoid pain and love will abandon you
for being insincere

Love must hurt for those who have
never been in love

For even those hurt in love,
love is still a bliss

I may muffle my thoughts
But how shall I command my heart
to not to fall?

So long were the days of pain,
that now I chase pleasures with a shame

How I wish to quiver in love again

MOONLIGHT

Printed in Poland
by Amazon Fulfillment
Poland Sp. z o.o., Wrocław

59173285R00092